Welcome to Christ Church Cathedral, Dublin

From whichever Christian tradition or other religious faith you come, you are welcome to this house of prayer. Even if you come without faith, we still hope you will find that the cathedral's ambiance and atmosphere will convey to you a sense of peace in a troubled world.

Christ Church is a Church of Ireland/Anglican/Episcopal cathedral, built *c.*1030. From its foundation it has been the spiritual heart of Dublin. St Laurence O'Toole is our patron and was the second archbishop of the diocese. The cathedral tries to follow his example of prayer and outreach to the dioceses of Dublin and Glendalough.

As you leave you will take with you something of our history and tradition. Being with us today has made you a part of that history, part of a building that has absorbed the prayers and stories of people and their lives for nearly one thousand years. You are truly welcome. Pray for us, as we shall continue to pray for you.

The Very Revd Dermot Dunne
Dean of Christ Church

Cathedral nave viewed from the east

A Brief History of Christ Church

The foundation of a Dublin cathedral dedicated to the Holy Trinity appears to have taken place some time after Sitriuc 'Silkbeard', Hiberno-Norse king of Dublin and Flannacán Ua Cellaig, king of Brega (north of Dublin) made a pilgrimage to Rome in 1028. The cathedral's relic collection bears the hallmarks of having been assembled in Cologne, a stopping point on the route where there were two houses of Irish Benedictines. It is most likely that the initial establishment of the Dublin cathedral was staffed by Benedictines, and subsequent bishops of Dublin were trained as such. By 1152, Dublin's Hiberno-Norse diocese, which for a time answered to Canterbury, was drawn into a reformed Irish church following the synod of Kells-Mellifont, which established Dublin as an archbishopric. The second archbishop of Dublin, Laurence O'Toole (Lorcán Ua Tuathail), former abbot of Glendalough and future patron saint of Dublin, introduced the rule of St Augustine to the cathedral priory, which remained in place until the Reformation.

The arrival of the Anglo-Normans in the 1170s altered both the culture and the fabric of the institution. Archbishop John Cumin, appointed in 1182, represented a new trend in the appointment of Englishmen, and he embarked on a rebuilding of the quire and transepts of the cathedral, including elaborately carved historiated capitals amidst Romanesque and some Gothic arches. The nave was later rebuilt in the mid-13th century to an early Gothic design, and can be compared with contemporary work at neighbouring St Patrick's cathedral down the hill. This rival church had been raised from collegiate to cathedral status in the early 13th century, which added a competitive edge to the architectural prowess of the two cathedrals, and to the appoint-ments of archbishops of Dublin. By 1300, in what must be a very rare occurrence, Christ Church and St Patrick's signed a 'composicio pacis', a peace agreement which acknowledged both institutions as diocesan cathedrals of the joint dioceses of Dublin and Glendalough (amalgamated in 1216).

The cathedral priory of Holy Trinity (or Christ Church, as it was less formally known from as early as the 1280s), went through a number of expansions during the medieval period including a new Lady chapel around 1230, an expanded presbytery in the 1280s and, most importantly, an extended quire in the late 1350s which moved the rood screen (the rood or crucifix was traditionally erected above it), to the eastern side of the crossing, and formed an enclosed quire which would survive until the 1870s. Numerous chapels occupied the nave and quire aisles, dedicated to St Nicholas, the Holy Trinity, St Edmund, king and martyr and St Laurence O'Toole, later rededicated to the Holy Ghost. Such was the proximity of the cathedral to Dublin castle that it was occasionally used for matters of state. A meeting of magnates held a parliament there in 1297, while in the 15th century, the Irish council frequently endorsed the appointment of a new governor in the cathedral's Lady chapel. Indeed the last chantry chapel erected in 1512 was an elaborate Gothic confection commissioned by the eighth earl of Kildare, Gearóid Mór Fitzgerald, who served as lord deputy almost continuously from 1477-1513.

Capitular seal of Christ Church

The grounds of the cathedral held an arrangement of buildings to house and feed the Augustinian canons. In the west range were the prior's chambers, while in the southern-most portion over an archway was the kitchen for both prior and canons. The south range consisted of the refectory where the canons ate in common, and in the eastern range adjoining the south transept was the dormitory, with the reredorter or toilets to the south. Beneath the dormitory was an elegant vaulted chapter-house, the ruins of which survive, dating probably to the late 1220s. The canons however were not just responsible for a small urban footprint, but for vast manorial estates of ecclesiastical land throughout County Dublin and beyond, leaving their names in such places as Deansgrange and Grangegorman. The main three were Clonkeen (Kill o' the Grange), Grangegorman (originally Killdulig) and Glasnevin, and the process of organising this property has been preserved in one of the longest chronological ranges of archival material in Ireland. Remarkably however, with the dissolution of the monasteries, Christ Church was the only institution to legally

survive, the crown and civic authorities complaining of the chasm that would be left by Christ Church's absence from the fabric of civic life. The cathedral simply adopted a secular or non-monastic constitution and the prior and canons became a new dean and chapter, a rebranding tactic that not only retained the same personnel but also saw the survival of their property holdings.

For some time afterwards, amid the ensuing liturgical and theo-logical developments of Edward, Mary and finally Elizabeth, the vicars choral continued to eat at a common table, but the realities of the post-Reformation world would soon encroach. First however, the cathedral experienced an architectural catastrophe in 1562 when the south wall of the nave collapsed, the roof falling with it. Rebuilding work was supported by the lord lieutenant, Thomas Radcliffe, and with the monastic order swept

away, the lords deputy and lords lieutenant at the castle began to frequent Christ Church more regularly. Sir Henry Sidney refurbished the quire in the 1560s very much as a royal chapel, and concurrently there was a rise in the number of funerary monuments to the new English governmental officials, replacing that of an older civic guard. With clergy being allowed to marry, the need for communal living also diminished, and the chapter was increasingly left with idle monastic buildings.

A new dean, Jonas Wheeler, in an increasingly Protestant chapter, set about reforming the cathedral and obtained a new charter from James I in 1604. He also solved the problem of the disused cloistral buildings in having the Four Courts of the judiciary moved into them in a refurbish-ment of 1608 by Samuel Molyneux, clerk of the royal works in Ireland. By the 1630s

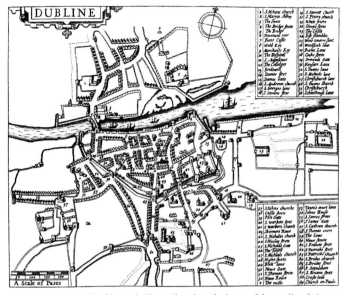

Speed's 1610 map of Dublin with Christ Church in the heart of the medieval city

14th-century recumbent effigies arranged here in 1570 to represent Richard fitz Gilbert de Clare, 'Strongbow', the leader of the Anglo-Normans, and his supposed son

View of the restored cathedral and synod hall with remainder of masons' workshop in foreground from The Graphic (4 May 1878)

under the influence of the lord deputy, Thomas Wentworth, the cathedral quire was restored to reflect the high-church Laudian sensibilities of the time, but this was not to last, and during the wars of the next decades on both islands, several Puritan congregations used the cathedral and its Lady chapel.

The Restoration of Charles II to the throne also saw two successive restorations of the quire of Christ Church, by now richly fitted out as a plastered, galleried space with classical detailing, and a centre of viceregal ceremony. In 1681, the dean of Christ Church, William Moreton, was consecrated as bishop of Kildare, a union of the two positions which was to endure until 1846. During the Jacobite rebellion of 1688-9, King James II attended Christ Church himself and appointed a new Roman Catholic dean, Alexius Stafford.

Following the battle of the Boyne in 1690 however, the status quo, and Bishop Moreton, returned to Christ Church, Stafford having been killed at the battle of Aughrim. The early years of the 18th century were marked by legal wranglings of precedence between the archbishop of Dublin and the dean of his cathedral, a quarrel continued by Moreton's successor, Welbore Ellis. The century was one of architectural and musical innovations however. The surveyor-general, Edward Lovett Pearce built a new deanery in Fishamble Street, sadly now demolished, while the cathedral's musical establishment flourished under the Roseingraves, Daniel (1698-1727), former organist of Gloucester, Winchester and Salisbury cathedrals, and his son Ralph (1727-47). It was at this time also, in 1742, that Händel's first performance of *Messiah* was given in Dublin by the choirs of St Patrick's and Christ Church

cathedrals, and both were involved regularly in society musical events throughout the remainder of the 18th century.

Signs of decline were in the offing by 1796 when the courts were removed to the quays, coupled with the city's expansion to the east which diminished the cathedral's centrality. The Act of Union in 1800 also saw the departure of considerable numbers of the aristocracy to London, and inevitably affected the already waning star of Christ Church as a royal chapel. A neo-Gothic restoration of the cathedral had been attempted in the late 18th century, but the building of the sophisticated neo-Gothic chapel at Dublin castle by Francis Johnston in 1814 sounded the death knell for Christ Church's claim to chapel royal status. At the same time the Wide Streets Commissioners were purchasing much cathedral land and demolished the houses on the north side of Skinners' Row, opening the cathedral's environs up to view for the first time. A belated restoration was undertaken by a relatively unknown architect, Matthew Price in 1831-3, completed in 1842-6, which was of questionable quality, and in any case the Irish Church Temporalities Act of 1833 was to strip the cathedral not only of its property but, on the death of Bishop Charles Lindsay, of its dean, when in 1846, the deanery was amalgamated with that of St Patrick's cathedral.

The year 1871, in which the Church of Ireland was disestablished, was also the year in which a large-scale restoration and rebuilding of Christ Church took place, undertaken by the English architect, George Edmund Street, and funded entirely by Henry Roe, a whiskey distiller, who ploughed his fortune into the project. Street took the opportunity to rebuild the Tudor south wall as a replica of the original north wall, and to replace the wooden roof with stone vaulting, resulting in the fine nave surviving today. He also demolished and rebuilt the nearby church of St Michael's, retaining its 16th-century tower as a synod hall for meetings of the Church of Ireland, and joined it by a dramatic bridge across the road to the cathedral. At the cathedral's eastern end he studied the ground plan of the crypt beneath and, so dismayed by the state of the long quire, had little hesitation in demolishing the structure and attempting a Victorian reconstruction of what the eastern chapels may have looked like - not original, but a work of art nonetheless.

In 1872, the deaneries of the two cathedrals were separated, and the archbishop of Dublin, a former dean of Westminster abbey, Richard Chenevix Trench, was appointed dean, a position which his successor William, 4th Baron Plunket retained until 1887, when he appointed a canon, William Conyngham Greene, as a dean separate from the archbishopric once more. The 20th century was, by and large, one of decline for Christ Church, with a dwindling Church of Ireland population keeping its head below the parapets following the establishment of the Free State in

Etching showing the south west view of Christ Church cathedral

1922. One later dean, E.H. Lewis-Crosby, a former chaplain to the lord lieutenant, nevertheless realised that the cathedral must be outward looking and did much to promote this former chapel royal in the new independent Ireland, emphasising its civic importance.

The year 2000 saw the publication of a cathedral history, *Christ Church cathedral Dublin: a history,* (available in the cathedral shop), the staging of an international liturgical festival and the restoration of the crypt.

The Friends of Christ Church Cathedral, established in 1929, supports worship and music in the cathedral and assists in its maintenance and repair, while drawing into fellowship all those who cherish Christ Church as part of Ireland's Christian Heritage

In addition to daily choral and said services, and to baptisms, weddings, funerals, confirmations, ordinations and consecrations, in recent years the cathedral has increasingly been in demand as a venue for lunchtime and evening concerts, while the crypt has also proved ideal for book launches, receptions and exhibitions. The year 2010 saw the cathedral taking a healthy interest in its past, with the excavation of a portion of the cloister garth, and in its future, with the relocation of the shop to the crypt and the opening of a cathedral coffee shop. Furthermore, as a venue, Christ Church has hosted numerous film, television, musical and cultural events, including the historical drama *The Tudors*, as well as festivals of classical and traditional music.

Victorian gothic chapter house door with decorated wrought iron hinges

Cathedral Precinct

The grounds of the cathedral today represent, with some deviations, the limit of the precincts (or liberty) of the medieval cathedral priory of Augustinian canons. This walled area contained the prior's house in the southwest corner (formerly occupied by the archbishop's palace), a chapterhouse, a cloister, canons' dormitories, and an eastern and western gate. In addition, throughout the 16th century, there developed a large-scale leasing of cathedral property for commercial uses, such as taverns, toy shops, wig-makers and the like. This cathedral liberty obtained a prestigious tenant in 1608, when the Four Courts of the judiciary were erected in the old cloister area using some of the disused monastic buildings. By 1631 there were so many inhabitants living within the precincts that the dean and chapter had to issue a set of orders which included instructions 'not to empty within the said Church yard or other open place of the said precincts, any Chamber pott, Ordure, Urine or other filth, garbage, durt or Ashes and that all Maisters, mistresses and parents shal be lyable and Aunwerable for the penalties of any of their servants or children'.

Ruins of the 13th-century chapter house

The departure of the Four Courts to Gandon's new building on the quays in 1796, coupled with the work of the Wide Streets Commissioners in the early 19th century, greatly reduced the importance of the cathedral liberty. In preparation for the visit of King George IV in 1821, Skinners' Row to the south of the cathedral was widened, the majority of the northern cathedral side was demolished and eventually Skinners' Row was renamed Christchurch Place. At this time, the Romanesque doorway in the north transept was moved to its present dominating position in the south transept. The original precinct plan was finally altered in 1886, when Lord Edward Street was built due east of the cathedral, creating a gentle curve from the truncated Fishamble Street to Christchurch Place.

The ruins which remain in the grounds today include a stump of stonework, on the right beneath the London Plane tree, which is the southeastern-most corner of the old long quire, all that remains of a mid-14th-century extension to the cathedral, demolished in the 1870s as part of the restoration project of George Edmund Street, the cathedral architect from 1868-82. The sunken ruin beside the south transept is all that remains of the 13th-century chapter house. Although damaged by fire in 1283, the building served the chapter until 1699. By 1794 it had been truncated and converted into a carriage entrance, and it was eventually demolished during the work of the Wide Streets Commissioners. Although Street was aware of the presence of the buried ruin during his 1870s restoration, it was his successor, Sir Thomas Drew, cathedral architect from 1882-1910, who excavated it in 1886. It was later restored in the 1980s by Dublin Corporation.

Cathedral Building

The deceptively Victorian appearance of Christ Church dates from the extensive rebuilding by Street from 1871-8. This included the erection of a synod hall (now the exhibition *Dublinia*) and a bridge linking it to the cathedral. Street's *forte* however, was in retaining the antiquity of the buildings which he was restoring: in the case of the synod hall, the incorporation of the old St Michael's church tower. Street proudly claimed his restoration of Christ Church to be *'a deed unequalled, so far as I know, in Europe'* and, despite using 3944 tons of freshly cut Caen stone, the amount of early Romanesque and early English fabric which he preserved should be rightly recognised as atypical of his time.

View of the cathedral and old synod hall in the background, now the Dublinia *exhibition*

Cathedral nave viewed from west

Nave

The nave which you see today dates from at least two periods: an early English phase (the north wall) which probably dates to the 1230s-50s. Street's restoration includes a mirrored south wall, the stone vaulting of the roof, the west wall and nave piers. The exquisitely proportioned design of the nave with its unusual joint triforia and clerestory levels, was a reflection of the ongoing competition with St Patrick's cathedral nearby which, as the largest building in medieval Ireland, could not be competed with in scale.

In 1562, the south wall and nave roof collapsed, probably also destroying the west window and wall. A crude, bare south wall without arcading, and a wooden roof, replaced them until the 1870s. Remains of the 1562 vault are still to be seen in the older stone springers supporting the north wall rib vaults, as well as in the angle at which it now leans, some 46cm out of plumb.

The 13th-century work in the nave is still surprisingly fresh. The foliate capitals on the north side of the nave are particularly noteworthy, especially the cheeky monkey-head stop on the third bay hood moulding. The bulk of the substantial nave piers is elegantly disguised by eight surrounding shafts, enriched by the deep recessing of the nave bay arches. The piers were dramatically reconstructed by Street in the 1870s. While this was being done, he supported the north wall on timber scaffolding. The nave is lit by a series of

Tomb commemorating Strongbow

simple neo-Georgian lights installed in 1999 which replace a variety of former models.

West Bay - Area A

The five-lancet west bay window, although a conjectural restoration, is an intelligent guess by Street as to its original 13th-century form. The north and south aisle windows depict (1) Daniel in the lions' den, (2) Adam's naming of the animals and (3) the death of Abel. The five-light west window depicts the tree of Jesse. The mural monument to the left of the west door commemorates Thomas Fletcher, dean and bishop of Kildare (d.1761), and overlooks a monument to Thomas Abbott (d. 1837), erected by the citizens of Dublin. The weeping child carved by Thomas Kirk, a well known Dublin sculptor, represents Abbott's connection with the Mendicity Institution. The monument to the right of the west door is to Samuel Auchmuty, an Irish colonel who fought in South America and Java in the 78th regiment of Foot of the

British army (d.1837), also by Kirk. All three monuments were originally banished to the crypt by Street during the 1870s restoration, but in 1910, following public outcry as to their inauspicious fate, they were moved to their present positions. More detailed information on the monuments can be found in a separate guide by Stuart Kinsella, which is available in the cathedral shop.

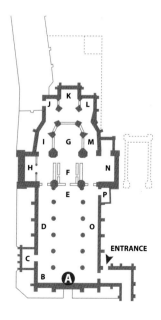

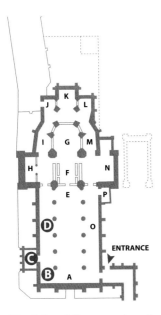

Musicians' Corner containing monuments to former cathedral musicians

Musicians' Corner - *Area B*

Here musicians of the cathedral are remembered. The tablets include a brass to the chorister, Edward Spring (d.1910, aged 29), a mural monument to Richard Woodward, organist of Christ Church and vicar choral of St Patrick's cathedral (d.1777). Sir John Stevenson (d.1833), best known for his adaptations of Irish melodies to the lyrics of Thomas Moore, is also commemorated. Vicar choral of Christ Church and St Patrick's, organist of Francis Johnston's chapel royal and master of the state band of musicians, he claimed to be the *'first native of Ireland admitted to office in the choir of Christchurch'*. There is no matching choirboy on the right because the unpaid sculptor withheld the final statue. To the right of the small trefoil-headed doorway is a brass to Sir Robert Prescott Stewart, perhaps the most ubiquitous of Dublin's 19th-century musicians (d.1894), who was professor of music at Trinity College, conductor of the choral society and organist of the chapel, as well as at Dublin castle's chapel royal and both Anglican cathedrals. A brass also exists to his successor, John Horan, who had been assistant to Stewart for 21 years (d.1908, not 1907 as his brass states). Finally, the Robinsons: Francis (d.1872), William (d.1881), John (d.1844), Joseph (d.1815) all sons of Francis (d.1834), pillars of the 19th-century cathedral music community, are remembered in a brass by Sawier of Dublin.

Baptistery - *Area C*

The original font was a simple octagonal bowl on a pedestal on the west side of the north-west pillar and is still preserved in the crypt. Street however built this antechamber to commemorate his wife, Jessie Mary Anne, who died during his work on the

Entrance to the baptistery

Stained glass window in baptistery dedicated to St Laurence O'Toole, former archbishop and patron saint of Dublin

cathedral. It is his one admitted deviation from the plan to restore the cathedral *'so that not an ancient stone which could be retained in its old place should be removed'*. It is a delicate, vaulted space supported by two sleek black marble columns which frame the lavishly decorated font with variegated marbles from all over Ireland. The five north windows commemorate Celtic saints: Cormac, Laurence O'Toole (patron saint of Dublin), Patrick, Cuthbert and Finbar. As Street's memorial, appropriately, those on the west are to Saint George and Saint Edmund while on the east, to the Blessed Virgin Mary and Saint Anne. Each was executed by Messrs Clayton & Bell of London.

View of the 13th-century north wall of nave from the south east

North Aisle - *Area D*

The arched entrance to the baptistery was originally one bay east prior to the 1870s restoration, and spanned an old northern entrance to the cathedral. The metal Canterbury cross to the right of the archway was a 1935 gift from the Friends of Canterbury cathedral to all the *'Cathedrals within the Empire'*, a present willingly displayed by Dean Lewis-Crosby, who was initially quite unhappy about Ireland's new independent status.

The windows of the north aisle include, from west to east: the blessing of Abraham by Melchisedec, and Noah's sacrifice and the appearance of the rainbow, erected by the Revd John Finlayson, prebendary of St Michael's, in memory of his parents. Beyond the baptistery, the windows depict Jacob's vision and Isaac bearing wood for his own sacrifice, Moses' descent from the Mount, Joseph taken out of the pit, David's victory over Goliath and the call of Samuel.

Vertical shaft dividing the bays of the nave, and uniting the nave pillars with the triforium and clerestory levels

surmounted Joseph Kirk's dignified sculpture of the bishop in the eastern-most window of the north aisle. After Lindsay's death the bishopric of Kildare was united with that of Dublin, while the deanery of Christ Church was united with that of St Patrick's. In 1871, following the disestablishment of the Church of Ireland, the deanery was again altered and united with the position of the archbishop of Dublin. The enamel, brass, marble and stone sculpture to Joseph Peacocke, archbishop of

Dublin, Glendalough and Kildare (d.1915) was designed in 1919 by R.C. Orpen, cathedral architect from 1910-*c.*1937, and contains the cathedral's sole 'arts and crafts' monument. This is the mitred crest within a seal of 'repoussé and champlevé enamel' by Oswald Reeves, one of Ireland's few proponents of the genre, whose work can also be found in a war memorial triptych preserved in All Saints' Grangegorman, a church within the cathedral group of parishes. Note also the strange wart-like feature on the column before the metal screen, which contrasts with the delicacy of the historiated Romanesque capitals in the transepts.

All of these nave windows are by Hardman & Son of Birmingham. Further information on the stained glass can be found in a guide by Lesley Whiteside available in the cathedral shop.

The third bay east contains a brass plaque to Charles Lindsay (d.1846), the last dean to hold the position of dean of Christ Church *in commendam* (i.e. together) with that of bishop of Kildare. The brass itself is transcribed from an older panel which prior to the 1870s

Circle of medieval pilgrims depicted in Victorian tiles in the nave copied from the surviving original

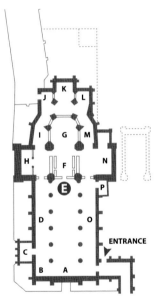

Screen - *Area E*

Immediately in front of Street's screen can be seen a number of items of interest: the pulpit of yellow Mansfield stone with the four evangelists surrounding it (including the bare-chinned Mark); the three-seated sedilia used by the clergy during the Sunday morning eucharist; and the Victorian eagle lectern used for the reading of the Bible, the

Cathedral quire screen

Victorian pulpit (above) and eagle lectern (below)

against the 'Romish' restoration of the cathedral. Particularly criticised was Street's depiction of the *Agnus Dei*, or 'Lamb of God' on the screen, beneath a replica of the cross of Cong.

To the right of the screen, note the capitals surrounding the eastern-most pillar, carved by the firm of Thomas Earp, Lambeth. These commemorate the archbishops of Armagh (Marcus Gervaise Beresford) and Dublin (Richard Chenevix Trench) who was also dean, as well as the funder of the restoration (Henry Roe) and its architect (Street). Four soaring grey pillars support the tower and belfry above, at the crossing of the transepts, quire and nave.

Quire - *Area F*

The quire is entirely Street's work. It replaces a long quire which in the 1280s was nothing more than the expansion of the chancel (the area of the altar) by about one bay. However, around the 1350s, Archbishop John de St Paul extended it by a number of bays, including a new east window, episcopal throne and probably also quire stalls. From this time, the nave (with the exception of the chantry chapels within it) was probably used less frequently, and was reserved primarily for preaching and prestige events. The most spectacular of these was the coronation of Lambert Simnel in 1487 as King Edward VI of England and lord of Ireland, with all its ensuing repercussions. Following the Reformation, the long quire acted primarily as a

spread wings of the eagle, St John's symbol, representing the dissemination of Christianity. This is also one of the better places from which to view the magnificent encaustic tiles with which the cathedral is floored throughout. Of sixty-four patterns in all, perhaps the 'foxy friars' caricatures are the most memorable (shown on previous page), reputedly depicting the friars who sought alms in the locality. Further information on the tiles is available in a separate booklet by Joanna Wren.

Prior to Street's restoration, the screen was one bay further east, surmounted by an organ, facing the crossing, the transepts and

nave making a clear T shape. The screen was not to the taste of many Church of Ireland evangelicals, including Canon Marrable who led the protests

The quire

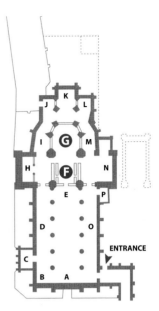

prestige church for both city and state, but by the early 17th century, following a period of Puritanism, it became more exclusively aligned with the crown. This culminated in Christ Church's position as chapel royal, confirmed in 1672 when, in a letter to the lord lieutenant, King Charles II referred to *'our said cathedral church and royal chapel'*.

The present quire occupies an area which, prior to the 1870s, was part of a spacious and unfurnished nave. The entrance is framed by two brass gates of exceptional craftsmanship by Potter of London, also responsible for the communion rails. The oak quire stalls were carved by Kett of Cambridge. The present lighting, installed in 1998, uses fibre optics, but the illumination of this space

in the 1870s was by means of an enormous central suspended brass candleabra (now removed), and those at the ends of the pews, holes for which still survive. The third row of stalls (and some of the second) is for the cathedral chapter, labelled as dignitaries, archdeacons, prebendaries and numbered canons. A stall on the south side (decani as it is known, derived from the dean's seat) was provided for Henry Roe as a *'slight acknowledgement of his rare munificence'* in restoring the building. The north side or cantoris, takes its name from the chantor, or precentor as this dignitary is known.

The archbishop's throne, a veritable rocket of gothic tracery work was designed by Street. To its left is the controversial brass

plaque to Archbishop William Conyngham Baron Plunket (d.1897) to which the 'ultra-Protestants' in the Church of Ireland were vehemently opposed because of crosses, since engraved over, on his scarf. The communion rail kneeler, commissioned from a Connemara firm by the Friends of Christ Church, features patterns from tiles throughout the building. The brass plaque to the left is to Plunket's predecessor, Archbishop Richard Chenevix Trench. The most recent addition to the quire is the Trinitarian plate in the oculus, the circular space in the crossing vaulting (2002).

Chancel - *Area G*

The chancel itself is one of the best positions from which to view the cathedral. It contains some interesting furnishings including a green marble retable behind the altar which may well be part of the *'magnificent altar...of one splendid slab of green scagliola,*

View of the quire with archbishop's throne (right) and, beyond the communion rails, the chancel with the altar (centre)

highly burnished' mentioned in an account of the long quire, *c*.1837. This would have been installed as part of an 1830s restoration of the cathedral of which Street did not approve and, if so, is an interesting survival. Also in the chancel is the 'abbot's chair' for visiting dignitaries, a table donated by the diocese of Cashel, Emly, Waterford and Lismore, and two chairs of particular note, one of Strawberry Hill Gothic vintage, the other 18th century, and apparently 'returned' from the chapel royal in Dublin castle in 1922. The stalls are from the former convent chapel of the community of St John the Evangelist, Sandymount, one of the only two women's religious orders ever to have existed in the Church of Ireland.

Architecturally, the chancel contains little of pre-Victorian date. Three 12th-century arches have been retained, those east of the crossing *in situ*, and that over the eastern arch removed from the north side of the old long

Late 12th-century historiated capital depicting musicians

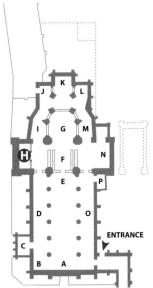

quire. This is interesting in itself, in that a plaster cast arch had survived on the south side as its match. Street's measurements of pillars in the crypt identified the northern arch as a perfect candidate for the eastern span, and so he presumed that it had been removed to the north side in the medieval period, a notable act of conservation. The remainder of the chancel is pure fantasy on Street's part, and enjoyable at that. He filled the spandrels of the arches with floriated diaper work in deep relief, and retained at least the notion of a joint triforium and clerestory. The 1870s vaulting matches the nave's in height, and is embellished with chevron over the altar, a feature picked up in

the diamond-decorated double-shafted columns in the arches on either side of the altar. The capitals are also worth inspecting, from the surrounding ambulatories.

North Transept - *Area H*

The north transept is a treasury of historiated Romanesque capitals executed during Arch-bishop Cumin's late 12th-century rebuilding. These include a pair of griffons clawing at human subjects and, led by a jester, a troupe of dancing musicians, whose swirling robes flow seductively and energetically. The delightful low vaulted space in the north transept consists of three quatrapartite vaults, and is a pleasant by-product of Street's relocation in 1878 of the Telford & Telford organ, which stood over the old screen where it had been erected in 1857. Unfortunately, the instrument was never satisfactory - Robert Stewart referred to it as a 'saw-sharpener' in 1881 - and despite a rebuilding in 1923 and 1960, it was not until 1984, when the present organ was built by Kenneth Jones of Bray under the guidance of Peter Sweeney, a former organist and director of music (1980-90), that the cathedral could claim to have an instrument of international calibre (restored 2004). A guide to the organ is available by Andrew Johnstone, a former associate organist of Christ Church (1995-2006).

Thanks to the gifts of Kitty (d.1982) and Brendan (d.1984) O'Brien, the west and east screens respectively were provided and the area used as a cathedral shop for almost twenty years. Today it is used as a private area of prayer. The icon to the Trinity which

adorns the east end, is after the medieval Russian painter, Andrei Rublev's Trinity, and was written by Georgeta Simion, wife of the Romanian Orthodox priest for the community based at Christ Church, Leeson Park. Also displayed is an exhibition of a sample of the cathedral's large selection of medieval stonework, curated by Michael O'Neill. Within the vaulted space is a number of fascinating monuments which include a floor slab lacking its brass inlay, possibly to Archbishop Richard Northalis (d. c.1397) and three unidentified floor slabs (two c.1400, and one 1544, the '4's being represented as truncated half-'eights'). Sir Henry Sidney, during his final term as lord deputy of Ireland (1575-78), contributed towards *'the building of the steeple and repair of the church'* for which his coat of arms was erected dated 1577, originally over the entrance to the north aisle, which was blocked up. Two floor slabs to Edward Goffe, merchant (d.1607) and his wife Margery, and Sheriff Richard Browne, lord mayor of

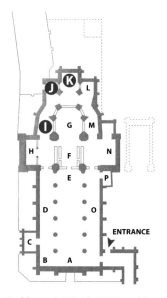

Dublin in 1605 (d.1615) and his wife, Margaret Staples are so similar in style to each other that they are probably by the same sculptor. A mural monument to Sir Edward Griffith (d.1540), records that he was barely in Ireland six months before he died. The floor slab fragment to William Wood (d.1650) is one of only three monuments to vergers in the cathedral. Wood was a stalwart member of the cathedral community, regularly witnessing leases, who owned a house in Ship Street nearby. Christopher Kerdiffe (d.1675), to whom a floor slab survives, came from an established Dublin family of scholars and clerics. The fine central mural monument to James Hewitt, Lord Lifford (d.1789), commemorates his twenty-two years as lord chancellor of Ireland, the longest holder of that position. His retirement plans were cut short though when, before he could resign, he caught a severe cold at the House of Lords and died.

Reflective space in north transept with icon of the Trinity

North Ambulatory - *Area I*

As you pass into the north ambulatory, observe the angle of the north wall of the Romanesque-chevroned archway. Note also the excellent preservation of the capitals, north and south, walled up for over 380 years. They include Romanesque examples of fruit pickers and beasts of the field on five sides of a blocky octagonal capital. Nearly all monuments in this area are of brass, commemorating among others, four bishops, three deans and three precentors.

The stained glass in this section of ambulatory (and indeed of quire and transepts) is by Messrs Clayton and Bell, and includes (left to right), the nativity (top), circumcision (bottom), the adoration of the magi (top), and the purification of the Blessed Virgin Mary (bottom). The next section includes Christ in the temple (top), and the flight into Egypt (bottom). The next window represents the baptism and temptation of Christ, while further east the window represents the Transfiguration, the entry into Jerusalem, the agony in the garden and the scourging of Jesus.

The civic pew can also be found in the ambulatory or nave aisle, upholstered in red velvet and featuring two brass fittings to hold the sword and mace of the city. The crest shows Dublin City Council's original crest, as the corporation of Dublin, three burning castles. The seat was restored in 1881 by the lord mayor of Dublin, George Moyers, and is still used by civic representatives.

Chapel of St Edmund, king and martyr

Chapel of St Edmund - *Area J*

In 1466, the guild of St Edmund was ordered to meet in the chapel of St Edmund to hear orders read bidding them provide themselves with, and practise themselves in, the use of bows and arrows. Located close to its original position, Street placed the chapel of St Edmund, king and martyr, in the north-eastern apse, an awkward liturgical space, as it also contains the 'cross' door which leads to administrative offices and the music and chapter rooms. It was furnished by the Girls' Brigade in memory of Constance Hall, secretary to their Dublin division from 1922-77. The Spanish majolica tiles by Street on the right wall are crowned by a Latin inscription in which Henry Roe dedicates all the stained glass in the chancel and transepts to his mother Catherine (d.1870).

Lady Chapel - *Area K*

The first Anglo-Norman Lady chapel was dedicated to St Mary of Whitland (*'Alba Landi'*) in Wales, but a new Lady chapel erected in the 13th century northeast of the cathedral served as the Lady chapel until the 1830s. The present chapel was designed by Street for meetings of the cathedral chapter. A nearby brass notes a refurbishment in 1977 by the St John Ambulance Brigade, in memory of Letitia Overend, but the present arrangement

Lady chapel with icons behind altar

dates to a reordering of 1999, that availed of the wall seats. The icons on the east wall are written by the Romanian-born iconographer, Mihai Cucu, and represent (along with their feast days): the Annunciation (25 March), the Visitation of Mary to Elizabeth (31 May), a triptych of Christ Pantocrator, the Incarnation (25 December) and the Resurrection (Easter Sunday). The modern lectern is in memory of William Mooney, and comes from the former church of St Mary's, Mary Street. The sculpture of the Madonna and Child is by Imogen Stuart and is placed on a reused stiff-leaf capital. Also preserved in the chapel is the old 'fount' or font stone which was originally built into one of the nave pillars near the northern entrance.

Chapel of St Laud - *Area L*

The dedication of this chapel to St Laud (or St Lo, St Loo, bishop of Coutances, 518) may be a result of a misreading of the afore-mentioned *'Landi'* as *'Laudi'*, but

Heart 'reliquary' associated with St Laurence O'Toole, second archbishop of Dublin

nevertheless, like the dedication to St Edmund, ultimately represents the personal piety of the Anglo-Normans. Worthy of note in this chapel is the heart traditionally associated with St Laurence O'Toole set in an iron heart-shaped casket, although few relics are known to have survived the Reformation. Born in Castle-dermot, County Kildare, in 1128, Laurence was abbot of Glenda-lough before being consecrated archbishop of Dublin in 1162. He died in Normandy in 1180, was buried at Eu in France, and canonised in 1225. The feast day of this patron saint of Dublin is

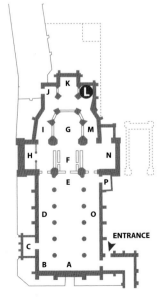

Medieval eagle lectern

14 November, and Wicklow heather can often be found beneath the heart. Note the medieval tiles which are preserved in this chapel. These survived in debris created by the collapse of the roof in 1562, were recovered from beneath the floor and reused by Street. He counted 64 different patterns, which he repro-duced throughout the cathedral: one Victorian commentator estimated the number of tiles to be 83,360. The chapel floor retains the original 'foxy friars' and a number of letters, which suggest the former existence of literary floor mosaics.

The medieval brass lectern in the form of an eagle, like its Victorian counterpart in the nave, was previously housed in the chapel of St Laud. It now forms part of the Treasury exhibition in the crypt. Accounts of 1542 surviving from the Augustinian cathedral priory describe a payment of 1 shilling and 6 pence for a year's worth of *'cleaning the eagle and both pair of great candlesticks'*. In the centuries since, it has had a wing replaced and an attempt to render it telescopic repaired. It has also survived a Victorian effort to make it appear wooden by painting it brown. Most recently it was restored by Mary Elizabeth Longfield in memory of her brother Robert Ormsby Longfield (d.1908).

South Ambulatory - *Area M*

The ambulatory has a two-window blind arcade, one of which contains an urn containing the ashes of Major Marko Zekov Popovich (d.1934), hereditary royal standard bearer of Montenegro who died in London and had been an acquaintance of Dean E.H. Lewis-Crosby. Nearby, and sometimes in the nave aisle the state pew can be found, exhibiting the arms of the house of Stuart taken from a former royal pew and restored by Henry Roe in 1882. Originally intended for the lord lieutenant or viceroy, today when it is used by the president of Ireland, the Irish harp is displayed in gold on a blue background draped on a flag over the old royal arms.

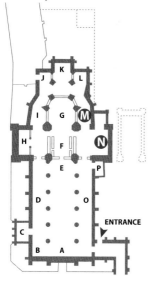

Transitional Romanesque-Gothic architecture in the south transept

South Transept - *Area N*

The south transept provides an excellent opportunity to examine Irish transitional architecture at the Romanesque-Gothic cusp. Under John Cumin's rebuilding, *c.*1186-*c.*1200, this portion of the cathedral was erected, along with the north transept, crossing and quire, probably following the ground plan of the crypt. The first storey, or triforium, butts into the base level of the above clere-story (literally 'clear storey' from a time when this storey would have been clear glass). Its interest lies in the fact that at triforium level, two pointed Gothic arches are contained within a round and chevroned Romanesque arch, thus marking a transition between architectural styles. The chapel of St Laurence O'Toole is an 1870s reconstruction. Prior to

Street's restoration this archway had been the entrance to the cathedral from Christ Church yard. While sinking foundations for the chapel in 1874, Street discovered a 13th-century tomb slab of a high-ranking lady, which is preserved on the south side of the chapel. An archbishop's tomb, thought by Street to be that of O'Toole, though now considered more likely to be that of John Cumin (d.1212) is in the northern niche. Behind the altar is probably the oldest inscribed monument in the building. It dates from the 14th century and commemorates John Lumbard and his family. The chapel window is a recent addition by Patrick Pollen, replacing an earlier window to the patron saints of Ireland, England, Scotland and Wales, SS Patrick, George,

Monument to the 19th earl of Kildare (d.1743)

Andrew and David. A brass on the chapel's north side commemorates Catherine O'Brien (d.1963) of 'The Tower of Glass' or 'An Túr Gloine', the studio associated with the works of Harry Clarke. The crucifixion in the transept's lower south window is one of the scheme's few individual dedications, presented by W.H.M. Ellis in memory of his wife Lavina (d.1876).

To the left of the St Laurence O'Toole chapel (used by the Mothers' Union), is a niche which formerly held a statue of the Blessed Virgin Mary, the crown from which was used in 1487 for the coronation of Lambert Simnel (p.18). The statue, whose hollowed out back was used at one stage as a horse's drinking trough, was the only one to survive the Reformation, and now rests in Whitefriar Street church. Today, the niche is occupied by a statue of Christ by Bertel Thorvaldsen, acquired by the Very Revd Harry Vere White, former dean of Christ Church (1918-21), during his time as

vicar of St Bartholomew's, a church which obtained its own life size version in 1921. Both statues were modelled on the original in the Vor Frue Kirke, the church (now cathedral) of Our Lady in Copenhagen. Of particular interest in the south transept are the monuments. These include the modern brasses such as that on the east wall to the Revd Norman Commiskey (d.1984), recast in 2007 to include his wife, Florence 'Florrie' (d.2004), and that on the corner belfry door erected by Lady Ada Charlotte Seeds-Kaye who restored the tower clock and chimes in memory of her first husband, Queen's Advocate-General, Robert Seeds (d.1892). Since 2000, the cathedral tower has held the greatest number of bells in the world, nineteen in all, that can be rung 'full circle'. Tours of the belfry can be made by arrangement.

The most impressive monument is Henry Cheere's masterpiece commemorating the 19th earl of Kildare, which features the first duke of Leinster among its 18th-century statuary. Note the unusual Kildare crest on the side, which features a monkey, supposedly responsible for saving the life of a Fitzgerald infant during a fire, and which is most likely a relic of the old Kildare pew.

Also note the monument erected in 1878 to the Victorian surgeon, John Hamilton (d.1857) and, on the other side of the doorway, the 16th-century monument to Francis Agard (d.1577) and his daughter, Cecilia Harrington (d.1584). Agard was a former secretary to Henry Sidney, twice lord deptuy, who referred to him as his *Fidus Achates*, a classical reference to faithful Achates, an intimate friend of Aeneas. The Latin inscription records Agard as *'a most sagacious Councillor of the Kingdom of Ireland for 26 years, during the reigns of Mary and Elizabeth'*. A successor of Sidney's as lord deputy is also remembered in the transept in an inconspicuous and rare 16th-century brass by the transept door. The 14th Baron Grey de Wilton, Sir Arthur Grey had this memorial erected in memory of his second and third sons who died in Dublin castle during his

Tudor alabaster monument commemorating Francis Agard (d.1577) and his daughter, Cecilia Harrington (d.1584)

lord deputyship (1580-2). Some other stone monuments nearby are almost indecipherable, but one might possibly be to Elizabeth Sidney (d.1567), the lord deputy's daughter, who died at his residence in Kilmainham and was buried in the cathedral, while another Gartered mural tablet with the initials H and S is probably to Henry Sidney himself. Two other monuments deserving mention are those to Dermot O'Brien (d.1945) who restored the steps of the transept, and Joe Coady, whose brass on the south side of the nave archway records his devotion to the cathedral for over 60 years, initially as sexton, and then as dean's verger from 1959 to 1987. The little Telford organ in the transept was the gift of Mrs Arthur Ellis and Canon Hogan, precentor in 1916.

South Aisle - *Area O*

The eastern-most window was erected by the 'Prince Mason of Ireland to the memory of Augustus Frederick, third Duke of Leinster, for 61 years Grand Master of the Order. *Born* Aug. 21, 1791; *died* Oct. 10, 1874'. The arms of the third duke of Leinster can be found in the stained glass surrounded by masonic emblems. Next is a window in memory of a medical doctor, Thomas E. Beatty (d.1872), probably a relative of Richard Beatty, master of the choristers (1830-73). Francis Robinson, Mus. D. and vicar choral at Christ Church, already mentioned in the musicians' corner (p.14), also died in 1872, and the window to him is visually musical in its composition. Finally,

the western-most window was 'Erected by the Rev. Precentor Seymour, M.A., in memory of his father (*ob*. 1870) his mother (*ob*. 1878) and his sister, Kate F. Seymour (*ob*. 1876)'. The clerestory windows in the nave represent the arms of the Irish dioceses and were executed by James Bell, Great Russell Street, London. They were designed by Street (whose address in 1868 was 51 Russell Square, London) from drawings by the Ulster king-of-arms, Sir John Bernard Burke. Exceptions to these are a window containing the arms of Henry Roe and, more surprisingly, the arms of the Welsh king, Gruffydd ap Cynan, raised in Dublin who, in 1137, left 20 shillings in his will to the cathedral.

The best known monument however is to Richard fitz Gilbert de Clare, alias 'Strongbow' (d.1176), and contrary to popular belief, not the earl of Pembroke since he was deprived of that title by Henry II in 1154. Best known for his leadership of the Anglo-Normans, he was

recruited as an ally by the exiled king of Leinster, Diarmait MacMurchada. As a nearby mural monument tells, this tomb was broken by the fall of the cathedral roof in 1562, and was re-erected in 1570 at the charge of Sir Henry Sidney. However, it seems that what was re-erected was another monument reputedly brought from St Peter's church in Drogheda and often considered to be the former lord deputy and seventh or eighth (depending on the authority counting) earl of Desmond, Thomas Fitzgerald, beheaded in Drogheda in 1468. Stylistically, however, the tomb belongs to the late 13th or early 14th century. The smaller monument beside 'Strongbow' is a genuine mystery. Feminine in form, it is unlikely that this was grand enough to have been a fragment of the original, or indeed that it might be his son (to which a dubious story of his being cleft in twain by his father for cowardice gave rise). This smaller tomb is also late 13th / early 14th century, but its association with the Strongbow monument

View of the south aisle

Medieval vaulting in the crypt

probably dates to the 1570s. On the opposite side of the pillar adjacent to Strongbow, note the deformed face on a capital secreted between two engaged shafts: a tragic figure or sculptor's prank? The capitals of the first pier at the west end of the aisle are composed of the evangelical emblems: the angel, the eagle, the lion and the ox.

Crypt - *Area P*

Monuments worth noting on the crypt stairs are to the Venerable John Torrens (d.1851) who, as archdeacon, held *in commendam* the rectory of the now vanished St Peter's church, Aungier street, and to James Elliott (d.1866), cathedral verger for 28 years, who is buried in Mount Jerome cemetery.

This spacious crypt bustled for many years with the noise of

business: alehouses, tobacconists, and much more, particularly during the 17th and 18th centuries when the nearby Four Courts brought activity to the cathedral precincts. Descending the steps, the first view is of a royal coat of arms surrounded by two statues.

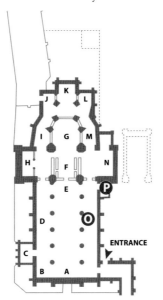

These items adorned the front of the old city hall or 'Tholsel' which stood opposite the cathedral until its demolition in 1820 whence they were removed to the crypt. The statues, in Portland stone, are of Charles I and II and are thought to be the oldest secular statues in Ireland. They were commissioned in 1683 by Dublin Corporation who engaged the Dublin-based William de Keyser, an 80-year-old Dutch sculptor.

Of another age and calibre is the monument (to the right) to John Bowes (d.1767). A major figure in 18th-century Ireland, Bowes

Monument to John Bowes (d. 1767)

was lord chancellor from 1757 and obtained a barony in 1758. The bas-relief head by John van Nost the Younger is recorded as being an excellent likeness. As a lord justice of Ireland, he was one of the most powerful men in the country, firmly opposed to relaxing penal laws. The monument is in two sections, having been moved from its original place against the south wall of the nave in the course of Street's 1870s restoration. Likewise, all the crypt monuments having been originally in the nave, are no longer proximate to their related burials.

Collection of Williamite plate

The eastern portion of the crypt dates from at least the late 12th, if not the late 11th century. At present it contains the treasury in which an impressive collection of the plate, reputedly given to the cathedral by William of Orange, is displayed along with the tabernacle and candlesticks from the last mass said in the cathedral under James II. Also on view is a rich collection of parish silver, as well as occasional exhibitions of books and manuscripts. The iron 'Armada' chest nearby is probably 17th century and although more likely to be a Dutch import, seems to have been purchased in 1689 and was used to send cathedral records to England to prevent them falling into Jacobite hands when they occupied the cathedral. The stocks, just outside the Treasury, date from about 1670 and were removed from their position in the cathedral yard (roughly where the chapel of St Laurence O'Toole is today) at the end of the 18th century. Power to use these belonged to the dean and chapter who could imprison offenders living within the precincts or liberties of the cathedral. The stonework behind

Cathedral stocks, c.1670

the stocks on the north side of the crypt crossing is a fascinating piece of architectural history whose completion date can be ascribed precisely to Thursday 17 May 1565. On this date, so the proctor, Peter Lewis, recounts, work was done on the *'fondacion of the stepull'* of which he was clearly proud, for he *'brought all the corrystores [choristers] to see the making of the fondacion and ewry of them brought a stone to the fondacyon and I bett [beat] them all that they myght ber in remembrance of the makyng of the work and I bestouyd apone the chyldryn, at dener tyme, j terstyn [a 16th-century Irish shilling]'*.

Nearby, is an impressive military monument to John Crawford Smith (d.1843), son of Robert Smith of Mountjoy Square, who was killed on active service in India fighting the army of Ammer Shire Mahomed, at Dubba near Hyderabad. A wide chronological range of monuments are represented in the crypt nave. This section of the nave dates from the early 13th century and still contains piers with carved Dundry chamfers. On the left William (d.1661) and Ambrose Cadogan (d.1693) are commemorated. William was secretary to the earl of Stafford in 1641 and major of horse, fighting under Cromwell against Phelim O'Neill and Owen Roe O'Neill in 1649. Ambrose Cadogan predeceased his father and was buried with William, his grandfather.

Further along, is a monumental slab to Gilbert Nicholson (d.1709) and his wife. In 1666, he replaced Thomas Howell as chapter clerk, and in addition became verger in

1668. Almost three decades later, in May 1697, he recorded his own resignation as verger and sexton, and later in the month, also resigned his position as registrar or chapter clerk. In the next bay is the morbid 'cat and rat', doomed forever to chase each other down an organ pipe. As James Joyce put it, *'as stuck as that cat to that mouse in that tube of that Christchurch organ'*, conserved in 2008 by the National Museum of Ireland.

To their right is the only monument in the crypt devoted to a woman, Margaret Jackson (d.1775), wife of Charles, bishop of Kildare and dean. Incidentally, she was also the daughter of a previous dean but one, Bishop Thomas Fletcher, already noted above (p.13). At the west end of the crypt nave are two monuments

Monument to Nathaniel Sneyd (d.1833)

to men who died violent deaths. Firstly, Lieutenant Colonel John Wallace King (d.1850 at Lahore in Pakistan), and the second to Nathaniel Sneyd (d.1833), a member of parliament for Cavan and a Dublin wine merchant. Sneyd was shot by the *'indiscriminating violence of an*

unhappy maniac'. It is probably the finest neo-classical monument in the cathedral and was executed by Thomas Kirk.

Moving east along the north aisle of the crypt, the cathedral shop and a new café, established in 2010 can be found. The shop contains a monument to Richard Laurence (d.1838), archbishop of Cashel, bishop of Waterford and Lismore, and a former regius professor of Hebrew at Oxford. In the floor nearby, under glass, are visible remains of an unidentified building on the site of the cathedral, possibly from the 11th-century cathedral, established by the Hiberno-Norse king, Sitriuc. The coffee shop contains a memorial to Bishop Welbore Ellis (d.1734), former dean, and his wife, Diana (d.1739) and family. Mrs Ellis's nose, broken during millennium conservation work, was expertly restored in 2002.

Nearby, is a tomb slab to a dean's vicar of both Christ Church and St Patrick's cathedrals, the Revd Robert Shenton (d.1798). Next to Shenton are two monuments with medical connections: the first commemorates George Renny (d.1848) who was director-general of the medical department of the army in Ireland. He died in the Royal Hospital, Kilmainham, and this monument was erected by the Royal College of Surgeons of Ireland. Henry Mathias (d.1849) was an assistant surgeon on H.M.S. Enterprise which was exploring the Arctic (as one might surmise from the evocative representation of ships and icebergs on his monument). He died at Port Leopold, Lat 74° N.

Further Reading

This guide reveals only a fraction of the diversity within the millennium-long history of the community associated with Christ Church.

Christ Church has probably had more publications written about it than any other Irish cathedral, certainly so far as contemporary writings are concerned. In recent years a considerable amount of research has resulted in a cathedral history and an ancillary series of seven cathedral documents (published by Four Courts Press), as well as a CD, all produced as part of a cathedral history project. Other works on the cathedral include a history of its music, collections of lunchtime lectures and a number of guides. We hope these kindle your interest in the cathedral and invite you to explore its history further.

Christ Church Histories

Kenneth Milne (ed.), *Christ Church cathedral: a history* (Dublin, 2000, 2010).

Barra Boydell, *A history of music at Christ Church cathedral, Dublin* (Woodbridge, 2004)

Christ Church Documents Series

(Series Editor: Raymond Gillespie)

The proctor's accounts of Peter Lewis, 1564-1565, ed. Raymond Gillespie (Dublin, 1996).

Account roll of the priory of the Holy Trinity, Dublin, 1337-1346, ed. James Mills, introduced by James Lydon and Alan J. Fletcher (Dublin, 1996).

The chapter act book of Christ Church Dublin, 1574-1634, ed. Raymond Gillespie (Dublin, 1997).

The registers of Christ Church cathedral, Dublin, ed. Raymond Refaussé with Colm Lennon (Dublin, 1998).

Music at Christ Church before 1800: documents and selected anthems, ed. Barra Boydell (Dublin, 1999).

Sing O ye heavens: historic anthems from Christ Church cathedral: a CD of anthems in performance, ed. Barra Boydell (Dublin, 1999).

George Edmund Street and the Restoration of Christ Church cathedral, Dublin, ed. Roger Stalley (Dublin, 2000).

Christ Church deeds, ed. M.J. McEnery & Raymond Refaussé (Dublin, 2001).

Collected Lectures on Christ Church

Stuart Kinsella (ed.), *Augustinians at Christ Church: the canons regular of the cathedral priory of Holy Trinity, Dublin* (Dublin, 2000).

Raymond Gillespie & Raymond Refaussé (ed.), *The medieval manuscripts of Christ Church cathedral, Dublin* (Dublin, 2006).

Guide Books

David Murphy & Leslie Taylor, *The bells of Christ Church Dublin* (Dublin, 1994).

Joanna Wren, *Floor tiles: a guide to the medieval and 19th century floor tiles of Christ Church cathedral, Dublin* (Dublin, 2003).

Lesley Whiteside, *The stained glass of Christ Church cathedral Dublin* (Dublin, 1999, revised 2010).

Andrew Johnstone, *Organs, past and present, at Christ Church cathedral* (Dublin: Christ Church cathedral, 2004), based on an article published in *Friends of Christ Church cathedral [Dublin] Newsletter*, 22:2 (Summer 2004), 20-2.

Stuart Kinsella, *Christ Church cathedral, Dublin: a survey of monuments* (Dublin: Christ Church cathedral, 2010)

Stuart Kinsella, *Visitor's guide: Christ Church cathedral, Dublin* (Dublin: Christ Church cathedral, 2003, revised 2012).

Acknowledgements

Text - Stuart Kinsella

Editorial work - Sarah Drumm, Ruairi Ferrie, Nuala Kavanagh

Design - DaVinci D&A

Photography - Liam Blake

Additional photography -

National Museum of Ireland:
page 3: carved Viking crook

Alan Banks:
page 3: coin
page 15: stained glass
page 16: nave bays
page 18: eagle lectern
page 23: Chapel of St Edmund
page 28: south aisle

Sarah Drumm:
page 25: medieval eagle lectern

Dr Stuart Kinsella is research advisor to the cathedral.